Sass & Sarcasm: The Art of Roasting Girls

The Writer Ullu

Published by Dark-Community Of Owl Publishing, 2024.

While every precaution has been taken in the preparation of this book, the publisher assumes no responsibility for errors or omissions, or for damages resulting from the use of the information contained herein.

SASS & SARCASM: THE ART OF ROASTING GIRLS

First edition. July 14, 2024.

Copyright © 2024 The Writer Ullu.

ISBN: 979-8224011056

Written by The Writer Ullu.

Table of Contents

Preface: Sass & Sarcasm: The Art of Roasting Girls (But Like, in a Totally Fun Way)

Hey there, witty warriors and queens of comebacks! Buckle up, because you're about to embark on a hilarious journey into the delightful world of sass and sarcasm, specifically targeted at, well, girls (but guys, you're welcome to crash the party too!).

Now, before you clutch your pearls and faint in horror (because fainting is so last season, darling), let's get one thing straight: this book isn't about mean-spirited barbs or leaving emotional scars. It's about the art of the playful roast, the kind that leaves everyone laughing (including the roastee, ideally).

Think of it as sharpening your wit like a diamond – cutting and brilliant, but used with precision and a dash of playful malice. We'll explore the art of the perfectly delivered comeback, the subtle jab disguised as a compliment, and the one-liners that land like a mic drop (because who doesn't love a good mic drop moment?).

But fear not, this isn't just a recipe book for verbal takedowns. We'll also delve into the power of self-deprecating humor, the importance of reading the room (because sometimes a well-timed silence is more savage than any insult), and the fine line between sassy and straight-up rude.

Remember, the goal is to have fun, flex your comedic muscles, and maybe leave your friends (or frenemies) slightly speechless (in a good way, of course). So, grab your sass supply, unleash your inner wit witch, and get ready to turn the world into your personal comedic playground. Because let's face it, girls who roast together, rule together (and probably have the most epic sleepovers ever).

NOW, LET'S GET THIS roasting party started!

Prologue: The Queen of Comebacks and the Curse of the Silent Stare

The cafeteria buzzed with the usual cacophony of teenage angst and lukewarm lunches. At a corner table, amidst a gaggle of giggly girls, sat Maya, the undisputed queen of the comeback. Maya's wit was as sharp as her eyeliner, her one-liners more lethal than a cafeteria tray of mystery meat.

Across from her sat Chloe, the perpetual target of Maya's playful jabs. Chloe, bless her heart, was as sweet as the artificially flavored juice boxes they served, and about as quick with a retort. Today, however, Chloe wore an uncharacteristic frown, her gaze fixed on a crumpled napkin in her hand.

"Earth to Chloe," Maya drawled, snapping her fingers in front of her friend's face. "Lost in the existential abyss of lukewarm tater tots again?"

Chloe flinched, her frown deepening. "It's not the tater tots," she mumbled, unfolding the napkin to reveal a scrawled message: "Your jokes are SO last year. Maybe consider silence for a change."

A collective gasp rippled through the table. An attack on Maya's wit was akin to a declaration of war. Maya's lips twitched, a dangerous glint in her eyes. Here was a challenge, a foe worthy of her comedic arsenal. The silence stretched, thick with anticipation. Then, a slow smile spread across Maya's face.

"Well, well," she drawled, her voice dripping with mock sincerity. "Looks like someone finally graduated from the School of Bland to the Institute of Insulting Inkwell Doodles. Impressive progress, Chloe, truly impressive."

The table erupted in laughter, even Chloe managing a small smile. The cafeteria fell silent, all eyes fixed on Maya. This wasn't just a comeback; it was a declaration. Maya, the queen of comebacks, had been challenged, but she emerged victorious, proving that even the sharpest wit can be disarmed by a little unexpected silence.

But something about the encounter lingered in Maya's mind. Perhaps it was the undeniable power of the silent stare, or maybe a glimpse of vulnerability in Chloe's eyes. Whatever it was, Maya knew this was just the beginning. The world of witty banter was about to get a whole lot more interesting, and maybe, just maybe, a sprinkle of self-awareness wouldn't hurt either.

This is the story of how Maya, the queen of comebacks, learned that the art of wit is more than just sharp words. It's about timing, about knowing your audience, and most importantly, about using humor to connect, not to conquer. Buckle up, roasters and roastees alike, because we're about to embark on a hilarious journey into the world of witty exchanges, where the laughter is loud and the lessons are even louder.

Acknowledgement

To our dearest readers, especially our wonderful female companions, we must begin by extending our sincerest apologies. This book, "Sass & Sarcasm: The Art of Roasting Girls," may have led you to believe that we, the authors, were embarking on a mission to equip you with the tools to mercilessly roast and tease our fellow females.

We assure you, this was never our intention. In fact, we hold the utmost respect for women and their incredible wit, strength, and resilience. We would never encourage anyone to use humor in a way that is hurtful, disrespectful, or exclusionary.

But wait, there's more! Just as you were about to forgive us for our seemingly insensitive book title, we unveil another twist. This book is not just about boys roasting girls; it's about the art of playful banter, the kind that can bring people together and create lasting memories.

And guess what? Girls are masters of this art. They've been roasting boys with their sharp wit and quick comebacks for centuries. So, we're here to say, "Bring it on, ladies!" We're ready to be roasted, teased, and challenged by your comedic prowess.

In the end, this book is not about dividing the sexes; it's about uniting them through the power of laughter. It's about learning to laugh at ourselves, to appreciate the humor in everyday situations, and to use our wit to connect with others in a positive and meaningful way.

So, let's put aside our differences and embrace the joy of playful roasting. Let's fill the world with laughter, one witty retort at a time. Because let's face it, life is too short to take ourselves too seriously. Especially when it comes to the art of roasting.

WITH HEARTFELT APOLOGIES and a sprinkle of mischief,

The Writer Ullu 😁

About D-COOP

Introduction

Introduction: Unleashing Your Inner Sass Master

Welcome, witty warriors and queens of comebacks! Have you ever dreamt of delivering a retort so sharp it could cut diamonds? Do you crave the satisfaction of leaving a friend speechless (in a good way, of course) with your perfectly timed quip? Then this book is your sass starter kit, your guide to mastering the art of the playful roast, specifically aimed at your fellow brilliant females (but hey, guys, feel free to join the fun too!).

Forget the stereotypical image of the "mean girl." We're not here to build walls with insults or leave emotional scars. This is all about wielding your wit like a glittering weapon: precise, polished, and deployed with a playful wink.

Here's what you can expect on this hilarious journey:

* The Art of the Comeback: We'll dissect the anatomy of a perfect retort, from the subtle jab disguised as a compliment to the one-liner that lands with the impact of a mic drop.

* The Power of Self-Deprecation: Because sometimes, the best way to disarm a situation is to poke fun at yourself first. Learn how to laugh at your own quirks and leave everyone in stitches.

* Reading the Room: Not Every Joke Lands: We'll explore the importance of gauging your audience and the delicate balance between playful teasing and genuine offense.

* Beyond the Burn: Wit as a Tool for Connection: Humor is a powerful social glue. We'll delve into how to use playful roasts to build rapport, strengthen friendships, and create unforgettable memories.

* The Evolution of Sass: From Playground Taunts to Polished Puns: We'll explore how to elevate your humor from childish jibes to witty wordplay and clever observations, leaving everyone impressed by your comedic prowess.

This book is your personal sass sensei, guiding you on your path to becoming a master of playful jabs and witty comebacks. But remember, with great wit comes great responsibility. We'll equip you with the tools to use humor with kindness and respect, ensuring your comedic barbs leave everyone laughing, not fuming.

So, unleash your inner sass master, dust off your vocabulary, and get ready to transform the world into your personal comedic playground. Because let's face it, girls who roast together, rule together (and probably have the most epic sleepovers ever). Buckle up, witty warriors – it's time to get schooled in the art of playful roasting!

Chapter 1: The Art of Wit: Mastering the Laugh Attack

Part 1

The Art of Wit: Mastering the Laugh Attack

Have you ever gotten the best of someone in a friendly conversation, leaving them laughing and admitting defeat? Or perhaps you've been on the receiving end of a witty remark that left you in stitches? Welcome to the wonderful world of wit, a cornerstone of humor and a powerful tool in communication.

This opening chapter dives into the art of wit, exploring what makes something witty, how to craft witty remarks, and the benefits of incorporating wit into your social interactions.

So, buckle up and get ready to unleash your inner humor ninja!

What Makes Something Witty?

Wit isn't just about telling jokes. It's about using language in a surprising, clever, and often times humorous way. Here are some key ingredients of wit:

* Originality: Witty remarks catch people off guard because they offer a fresh perspective or unexpected twist on a familiar situation.

* Brevity: Conciseness is key. Witty remarks are like mini-bombs of laughter that explode in a short burst, leaving a lasting impact.

* Relevance: The best wit is targeted. It references the situation at hand or something the other person has said, making it more impactful and engaging.

* Delivery: Timing and tone are crucial. A perfectly timed witty remark can elevate a conversation, while a fumbled delivery can fall flat.

CRAFTING WITTY REMARKS: Your Verbal Toolkit

Now that you know the hallmarks of wit, let's explore some techniques to craft your own witty remarks:

* The Observational Approach: Pay close attention to the world around you. Notice quirks, ironies, and funny details in everyday situations. Use these observations to craft witty remarks that highlight the humor in the ordinary.

* The Playful Jab: Friendly teasing can be a great way to add wit to your conversations. Just remember to keep it lighthearted and avoid anything that could be hurtful or offensive.

* The Wordplay Twist: Puns, metaphors, and other forms of wordplay can add a layer of wit to your remarks. But be mindful not to overuse them, or your humor might become convoluted.

* The Pop Culture Reference: A well-timed pop culture reference can be a great way to add humor and demonstrate that you're in tune with current trends. Just make sure the reference is relevant to the conversation and that everyone understands it.

THE BENEFITS OF BEING Witty

Wit isn't just about getting laughs (although that's definitely a perk). Here are some additional benefits of incorporating wit into your communication:

* Boosts Confidence: Delivering a witty remark can be a confidence booster. It shows that you're quick on your feet and can think creatively.

* Strengthens Relationships: Wit can be a powerful social tool. It helps you connect with others, build rapport, and create a sense of camaraderie.

* Sharpens Communication Skills: Wit requires you to think on your feet and react quickly. This constant mental exercise hones your communication skills and makes you a more effective communicator overall.

So there you have it! Wit is a valuable tool that can add humor, charm, and depth to your communication. By understanding its core principles and practicing these techniques, you can become a master of the witty remark, leaving your friends and colleagues rolling in the aisles.

Part 2

The Roasting Arsenal: Tools for a Witty Delivery

Now that you've grasped the essence of wit, let's delve into the tools you need to deliver it effectively. Here's your witty arsenal:

* Knowledge is Power: A well-stocked mental library is a must. The more you know about various subjects, pop culture references, and current events, the more opportunities you'll have to craft witty remarks.

* Practice Makes Perfect: Don't be afraid to experiment and practice your wit. Engage in playful banter with friends, participate in online forums known for witty exchanges, or try your hand at stand-up comedy (open mic nights can be a great training ground).

* Observation is Key: As mentioned earlier, hone your observational skills. Pay attention to the people around you, their mannerisms, quirks, and speech patterns. This provides a treasure trove of material for witty remarks tailored to the situation and individual.

BUILDING YOUR DELIVERY Chops

Witty remarks can lose their impact with a poor delivery. Here are some tips to ensure your humor lands:

* Timing is Everything: A well-timed witty remark can elevate a conversation, while one that arrives too late or too early can fall flat. Learn to read the room and wait for the perfect pause or conversational lull to unleash your witty quip.

* Vocal Variety is Key: Avoid a monotone delivery. Inflection, volume control, and a touch of theatricality can add emphasis to your witty remark and make it even funnier.

* Confidence is King (or Queen): Project confidence even if you're feeling a bit nervous. A self-assured delivery will make your witty remark even more impactful. Remember, even if the joke itself isn't a homerun, your confidence can win over the audience.

* Body Language Matters: Your body language complements your verbal delivery. Maintain eye contact, use expressive gestures (but avoid being overly dramatic), and smile to show you're having fun.

Practice Makes Perfect: Exercises to Hone Your Wit

Here are some exercises to sharpen your wit and become a master of the laugh attack:

* The Headline Challenge: Pick up a newspaper or scroll through online news headlines. Try to rewrite them in a witty or humorous way. This exercise forces you to think creatively and identify the inherent humor in everyday situations.

* The Caption Master: Browse through funny images or memes online. Craft witty captions that enhance the humor of the image. This will help you think visually and write concise, impactful remarks.

* The Movie Misquote: Take a well-known movie quote and rewrite it in a witty or nonsensical way. This is a fun way to play with language and explore the absurdity of humor.

REMEMBER, WIT IS A skill that develops over time. The more you practice, observe, and experiment, the more comfortable and confident you'll become in wielding the power of humor in your communication.

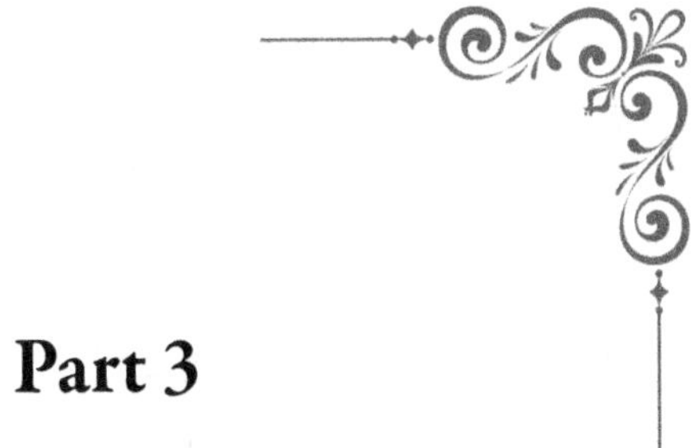

Part 3

The Roasting Rules: Etiquette for the Verbally Volleys

Wit can be a powerful tool, but like any powerful tool, it needs to be wielded responsibly. Here's where etiquette comes in. We don't want your witty remarks to leave someone feeling hurt or excluded.

* Know Your Audience: Tailor your wit to the person you're interacting with. What one friend finds funny, another might find offensive. Be mindful of cultural sensitivities and avoid humor that relies on stereotypes or prejudices.

* Punch Up, Not Down: Witty remarks are best used to playfully tease equals or superiors (think friendly banter with a colleague or a light jab at a boss who can take a joke). Avoid using wit to target those in a weaker position or those who may be easily offended.

* The One-Liner Wonder: Keep it short and sweet. A barrage of witty remarks can become overwhelming and exhausting for the listener. Aim for one or two well-placed witty remarks to maximize their impact.

* Leave Room for Reply: Witty remarks should spark conversation, not shut it down. Leave space for the other person to respond and engage in a humorous back-and-forth.

* The Art of the Apology: If your witty remark lands badly, be prepared to apologize sincerely. Acknowledge that your humor missed the mark and move on.

THE POWER OF SELF-DEPRECATION

Self-deprecating humor can be a great way to disarm others and deflect potential offense. A well-timed witty remark about your own shortcomings can endear you to others and show that you can laugh at yourself.

Witty Banter vs. Mean-Spirited Barbs

The key difference between witty banter and mean-spirited barbs lies in intent. Witty banter is playful and good-natured, while mean-spirited barbs are intended to hurt or belittle the other person.

Here are some signs your humor might be crossing the line:

* The other person seems withdrawn or uncomfortable.

* The laughter feels forced or awkward.

* The conversation grinds to a halt after your witty remark.

If you notice any of these signs, it's best to apologize and change the subject.

THE IMPORTANCE OF RESPECT

Wit should be used to build rapport and create a sense of camaraderie, not to tear someone down. By respecting your audience and using wit responsibly, you can ensure your humor lands effectively and leaves everyone laughing.

With these guidelines in mind, you're well on your way to becoming a master of the witty remark, ready to engage in playful banter and leave your mark as a humorous conversationalist. In the next part, we'll delve into the world of comedic heroes and explore the history and legacy of roasting in popular culture.

Part 4

The Roasting Hall of Fame: Legends Who Lit Up the Stage Witty banter and playful jabs have a long and illustrious history. From the comedic giants of the past to the modern-day masters of the roast, these legendary figures have paved the way for the art of witty discourse. Let's celebrate some of the iconic roasters who have left their mark on comedy:

* Oscar Wilde (1854-1900): The Irish writer and playwright was famous for his sharp wit and epigrams. His barbs were often laced with social commentary and a touch of cruelty, but his undeniable talent for wordplay made him a master of the cutting remark.

* Dorothy Parker (1892-1967): An American poet, critic, and satirist, Dorothy Parker was known for her acerbic wit and sharp observations on society. Her cutting remarks and witty one-liners were legendary, making her a formidable figure in the New York literary scene.

* Muhammad Ali (1942-2016): The iconic boxer wasn't just a force in the ring; he was also a master of self-promotion and playful trash talk. His witty poems, taunts, and predictions aimed at his opponents not only got under their skin but also entertained audiences and solidified his place as a charismatic showman.

* Johnny Carson (1925-2005): The king of late-night talk shows, Johnny Carson, was a master of observational humor and witty banter. His monologues poked fun at current events and celebrities, all delivered with a smooth, unflappable style that made him a household name.

* David Letterman (born 1941): Another late-night legend, David Letterman, took a more sardonic and acerbic approach to wit. His monologues and interviews were filled with witty barbs and unexpected jokes, making him a favorite among fans who enjoyed his dark humor.

* Joan Rivers (1933-2014): A true pioneer of female comedians, Joan Rivers was known for her brash, no-holds-barred humor. Her celebrity roasts were legendary, filled with cutting jokes and outrageous observations that pushed the boundaries of comedic taste.

* Jeff Ross (born 1953): A modern-day roast master, Jeff Ross has become synonymous with the art of the comedic diss. His jokes are often shocking and politically incorrect, but his undeniable talent for wordplay and comedic timing keeps audiences laughing, even when they're wincing.

These are just a few examples of the many talented comedians and personalities who have mastered the art of wit and comedic roasting. Their legacies inspire us to use humor creatively, engage in playful banter, and find humor in everyday situations.

By understanding the history and techniques of wit, you can incorporate it into your own communication style. In the following chapters, we'll explore how wit can be applied to various situations, from navigating everyday life to dissecting pop culture trends. So, the next time you find yourself in a conversation, remember the tools and techniques you've learned, and unleash your inner wit! You might just surprise yourself and leave everyone around you in stitches.

Chapter 2: Roasting the Everyday: Finding Humor in the Mundane

Part 1

Life isn't all sunshine and rainbows. There's the morning struggle to hit snooze one too many times, the awkward social blunders, and the never-ending quest for that perfect outfit. But hey, that's where the beauty of roasting comes in! By applying a touch of wit and humor to these everyday situations, you can not only navigate them with grace but also find laughter and amusement along the way.

The Roasting Ritual: From Bedhead to Burnt Toast

* The Rise and Grind (or Shouldn't It Be Snooze and Hide?):

* Target the struggle of mornings with relatable roasts about the battle with the alarm clock, the search for that elusive lost sock, and the questionable fashion choices fueled by sleep deprivation.

* Example: "Looking like you wrestled a flock of pigeons for your clothes in the dark. Maybe hit snooze just a tad too many times this morning?"

* The Commuting Catastrophe:

* Roasting the chaos of public transport or the never-ending traffic jam can turn a frustrating experience into a shared chuckle.

* Example: "That bus must be running on the tears of dreams – seems like it's never going to get here! Maybe you should have

trained your pet snail to take you to work – it would probably be faster."

* The Coffee Conundrum:

* Everyone loves a good cup of coffee, and the quest for that perfect caffeine fix can be a source of amusement.

* Example: "Is that even coffee anymore, or did you accidentally brew yesterday's newspaper? Maybe add a double shot of espresso – you look like you could use the energy boost!"

Roasting Your Roommates and Family: Keeping it Lighthearted

* The Kitchen Chronicles:

* A messy kitchen or an empty fridge can be opportunities for some lighthearted roasting amongst housemates or family.

* Example: "Who left that science experiment growing in the back of the fridge? Pretty sure it wasn't there yesterday. Maybe label your food next time – science project vs. last night's leftovers?"

* The Chore Charade:

* Dodge the blame for those neglected chores with a witty quip. But remember, keep it light and playful – the goal is to share a laugh, not start a war.

* Example: "Wow, those dust bunnies are multiplying faster than rabbits! Maybe they should be the ones doing the chores around here. At least they seem more motivated!"

Turning Errands into Entertainment

* The Shopping Spree (or Struggle):

* Lost in the clothing labyrinth or overwhelmed by grocery store choices? A bit of self-deprecating humor can ease the tension.

* Example: "Do clothes multiply when you're not looking? Why can I never find anything in this store? Maybe I should just wear a giant question mark on my shirt – 'Is this what I'm looking for?'"

* The Bank Statement Blues:

* Let's face it, bank statements can be a source of mild panic. A touch of humor can help you (and your friends) cope with the reality of your spending habits.

* Example: "Pretty sure this bank statement is trying to tell me something in Morse code – all I see are red squiggly lines! Maybe it's time to switch to a ramen noodle budget."

By incorporating these roasting techniques into your daily routine, you can find humor in the mundane and transform everyday situations into opportunities for laughter and connection. Remember, roasting is all about playful jabs and witty observations – it's not about being mean-spirited or hurtful. So, the next time you're stuck in traffic or battling a messy kitchen, unleash your inner roastmaster and find the funny side!

Part 2

The Social Scene: Roasting Your Way Through Awkward Encounters

Social interactions aren't always smooth sailing. There are awkward silences, name mispronunciations, and those unforgettable party blunders. But fear not, for the art of roasting can be your secret weapon in navigating these situations with grace (and maybe a little laughter).

* The Name Game:

* Awkwardly forgetting someone's name? A witty remark can acknowledge the slip-up and lighten the mood.

* Example: "Sorry, my brain is on vacation today! Maybe I should give you a nickname – Captain Awkward seems fitting after that one. What do you think?"

* The Small Talk Struggle:

* Stuck in a conversation filled with generic questions about the weather? A playful jab can break the ice and lead to more interesting topics.

* Example: "So, how's the weather doing its usual thing? Maybe we should skip the small talk and move on to the truly important questions – like what's the best pizza topping?"

* The Party Blunder:

* Did you spill your drink or accidentally trip over your own feet? Embrace the awkwardness with a self-deprecating roast that shows you can laugh at yourself.
* Example: "Wow, I think I owe the dance floor an apology for that move. Maybe I should stick to sitting down and telling embarrassing stories – I seem to be a natural at those!"
Roasting Your Dates (the Nice Way):
* The Dinner Date Debacle:
* A spilled drink or a funny food mishap can turn into a shared laugh if you handle it with a touch of humor.
* Example: "Looks like I have a newfound talent for synchronized swimming – with my napkin! Maybe this is a sign we should order dessert first – seems like things are getting messy already."
* The Movie Mishap:
* Picked a truly awful movie for your date? A lighthearted roast can acknowledge the dud and maybe lead to a fun discussion about the worst movies ever made.
* Example: "Pretty sure this movie is auditioning for a spot in the 'Worst Films Ever Made' hall of fame. Maybe we should write our own hilarious commentary throughout – it could be more entertaining than the actual movie!"
Roasting Your Friends (Because That's What Friends Do):
* The Fashion Faux Pas:
* Your friend's outfit is a bit, well, questionable? A gentle roast can be a way of showing you care (and maybe offer a friendly wardrobe intervention).
* Example: "Hey, that outfit is...unique! Are you auditioning for a role in a time travel movie? Maybe I should lend you a jacket – this one seems like it got lost in the 80s."

* The Competitive Spirit:
* A little friendly competition can be fun, but sometimes it gets out of hand. A playful roast can remind everyone to keep things light.
* Example: "Woah there, slow down champ! You're making the rest of us look bad. Maybe we should give you a participation trophy – just kidding (or maybe not)!"

Remember, the key to social roasting is to keep it lighthearted and good-natured. Target the situation, not the person, and always be prepared to laugh at yourself. By using humor this way, you can navigate even the most awkward social situations and strengthen your bonds with friends and acquaintances.

Part 3

The Academic Arena: Turning Study Struggles into Witty Remarks

Ah, student life. A time of late nights, mountains of textbooks, and professors who seem to speak a language entirely different from English (or whatever your native language may be). But fear not, weary scholar! Even in the depths of academic despair, humor can be your saving grace. Here's how to use wit to navigate the challenges of student life:

* The Pre-Exam Panic: Surrounded by mountains of notes and fueled by caffeine, pre-exam jitters are a real thing. A touch of self-deprecating humor can ease the tension and remind yourself (and maybe your classmates) that everyone feels the pressure.

* Example: "Pretty sure my brain is officially fried from all this studying. I think I just saw my textbook blink at me. Maybe I should wear a helmet to the exam – just in case knowledge overload happens."

* The Professorial Ponderings: Professors can be brilliant minds, but their lectures can sometimes feel like they're delivered in a different language. A witty remark (delivered silently in your head, of course) can help you stay focused and even spark a healthy debate later.

* Example: "Did the professor just invent a new word, or did I accidentally slip into a parallel universe where everyone speaks in riddles? Maybe I should take notes in hieroglyphics – seems just as clear at this point." (Remember, this is just for your amusement, not for public display!)

* The Group Project Mishaps: Group projects can be a breeding ground for frustration and arguments. A touch of lighthearted roasting can help break the tension and remind everyone to keep things civil (while still getting the work done).

* Example: "So, who wants to explain why there are only three paragraphs written in this 10-page document? Maybe we should assign roles – comedian, writer, and sleep-deprived coffee runner. Seems like we've got all the bases covered!"

Roasting Your Fellow Students (the Friendly Kind):

* The Procrastination Pro: We've all been there – putting off an assignment until the last minute. A friendly roast can remind your fellow procrastinator to get on track (and maybe inspire some solidarity in your shared struggle).

* Example: "Hey, is that the sound of the deadline approaching at breakneck speed? Maybe you should put down that social media feed and pick up a textbook. Unless, of course, you're aiming for the 'all-nighter champion' award."

* The Sleep-Deprived Study Buddy: Fueled by caffeine and fueled by sheer willpower, sleep-deprived study sessions are a common student experience. A playful jab at your study buddy's exhaustion can be a way to acknowledge the struggle and keep each other motivated.

* Example: "Whoa, those bags under your eyes are starting to develop their own zip code! Maybe we should invest in some extra-strength coffee and bright lights – this library needs a

serious wattage upgrade if we're going to survive this study session."

Turning Tests into Triumphs:

* The Post-Exam Debrief: Exams are over, and it's time to compare notes and anxieties. A witty remark about the exam's difficulty can turn into a shared laugh and a celebration of surviving another academic hurdle.

* Example: "Pretty sure that exam was designed by a sadistic genius. I think I saw a question that required knowledge of ancient Babylonian basket weaving techniques. Maybe we should all get participation trophies – just for showing up and not crying."

By using wit in these situations, you can not only relieve stress but also build camaraderie with your fellow students. Remember, humor is a powerful tool that can help you navigate the challenges of student life and create lasting memories along the way.

Part 4

The Fashion Fiesta: Roasting Your Way Through Wardrobe Mishaps

The world of fashion is a vast and sometimes confusing landscape. Trends come and go faster than you can say "haute couture," and even the most fashion-forward among us can have a wardrobe malfunction or two. But fear not, fellow fashionistas (and those who are, ahem, fashion-challenged)! With a touch of wit, you can navigate even the most questionable fashion choices and turn them into opportunities for laughter.

* The Mismatched Masterpiece:

So your outfit seems like it belongs in different decades or design galaxies? Embrace the clash with a self-deprecating roast that acknowledges the avant-garde nature of your ensemble.

* Example: "Feeling like a walking art exhibit today! Maybe the Museum of Modern Mismatched Fashion would be interested in acquiring this piece. What do you think – title it 'Ode to Accidental Stripes'?"

* The Brand Name Blunder:

Fell victim to a knock-off designer item? A playful jab at the questionable brand name can be more amusing than denial.

* Example: "Pretty sure this bag is a collaboration between 'Louis Vuitton' and 'Slightly Off-Brand Luigi.' Maybe it's the

limited-edition 'Faux Fancy' collection! But hey, at least it holds my stuff, right?"

* The Comfort Over Couture Conundrum:

Sometimes, comfort wins over style. A lighthearted roast of your own outfit choices can be a way to celebrate prioritizing comfort (even if it means sacrificing a bit of fashion sense).

* Example: "Rocking the 'Grandma Chic' look today! These sweatpants may not be runway-ready, but they sure are comfortable. Maybe I'll add a tiara and call it 'Comfy Couture.'"

Roasting Your Friends' Fashion Faux Pas (the Gentle Kind):

* The Outrageous Trend Follower:

Your friend is rocking the latest, most outlandish trend? A playful roast can acknowledge their fashion bravery (even if you secretly think it's a bit much).

* Example: "Woah, that outfit is definitely a statement piece! Maybe a little too loud for the library, but hey, at least you're not blending in with the beige background. You're like a walking rainbow – gotta appreciate the commitment!"

* The Stuck-in-a-Rut Rut:

If your friend seems stuck in a fashion rut, a gentle (and constructive) roast might be the nudge they need to experiment a bit.

* Example: "Is that the same outfit I saw you wearing last week (and the week before that)? Maybe it's time to shake things up a bit! We could have a 'Wardrobe Rescue' intervention and create some fresh looks."

Turning Fashion Fails into Fun:

By using wit in these situations, you can not only navigate fashion faux pas with humor, but also create hilarious memories with your friends. Remember, fashion is about having fun and expressing yourself. So, don't be afraid to laugh at yourself and others (in a good-natured way) when it comes to your wardrobe choices. Embrace the mismatched, the questionable, and the downright comfy, and turn them into opportunities for laughter and self-expression.

Chapter 3: Roasting the Realm of Entertainment: From Sitcoms to Silver Screens

Part 1

The world of entertainment is a vast playground filled with hilarious sitcoms, tearjerking dramas, and action-packed blockbusters. But even the most dedicated couch potato or movie buff can find themselves facing moments of questionable plotlines, cringe-worthy acting, and special effects that would make a five-year-old giggle. Fear not, fellow entertainment enthusiasts! With your newly honed wit, you can dissect these moments with humor and turn them into opportunities for laughter and insightful critique.

The Sitcom Skewering: Roasting Your Favorite Shows

* The Laugh Track Letdown: The laugh track, a staple of sitcom history, can sometimes feel intrusive or misplaced. A witty remark about the overly enthusiastic laughter can add humor to the moment.

* Example: "Did that joke just land with a resounding thud? Maybe the laugh track needs a vacation. This silence is starting to feel more comedic than the actual punchline."

* The Predictable Plot Twist: Sitcoms often rely on predictable formulas and plot twists. A playful jab at the show's lack of originality can be a way to acknowledge the cliche while still enjoying the show.

* Example: "Whoa, saw that plot twist coming a mile away! Pretty sure it was telegraphed by a flashing neon sign and a dramatic music cue. But hey, at least we know what to expect – comfort food for the funny bone."

* The Cast of Characters:

From the lovable goofball to the sassy best friend, sitcom characters often fall into familiar archetypes. A witty observation about these character traits can add a layer of humor to your viewing experience.

* Example: "Is it just me, or is the quirky neighbor lady channeling her inner squirrel this episode? Maybe she should invest in some nuts – seems like she's forgotten how to act human again."

Roasting Reality TV: The Guilty Pleasure with a Punchline

* The Staged "Reality": Let's face it, reality TV isn't always as real as it seems. A playful roast at the show's manufactured drama can add a dose of humor to the often-absurd situations.

* Example: "Pretty sure this fight scene was choreographed by a team of Hollywood stunt people. And is that a tear rolling down your cheek, or did someone just spray you with a water bottle? This drama is more staged than a Broadway musical."

* The Fame-Obsessed Cast:

Many reality TV stars are driven by a desire for fame and fortune. A witty observation about their self-absorption can be a way to acknowledge the absurdity of the situation.

* Example: "Is that contestant staring into the mirror again? Pretty sure they've memorized every angle of their face by now. Maybe they should invest in a selfie stick – seems like they're obsessed with capturing their own 'perfection.'"

* The Outrageous Challenges:

Reality TV thrives on outrageous challenges designed to push contestants to their limits. A sarcastic jab at the absurdity of these challenges can be a way to add humor to the often-grueling tasks.

* Example: "So, they're making them eat bugs for a million dollars? That's definitely not on my career bucket list. Maybe I should just stick to watching them suffer (and hopefully laugh) from the comfort of my couch."

Turning Entertainment into Witty Commentary

By using wit in this way, you can become a master of dissecting entertainment. You'll learn to appreciate the humor in the familiar, find amusement in the predictable, and expose the absurdity of the staged. Remember, your witty remarks should be delivered with a playful spirit and a love for the entertainment you're roasting. So, grab your remote, settle in for your favorite show, and unleash your inner entertainment critic with a touch of wit!

Part 2

The Silver Screen Savaging: Poking Fun at Blockbusters and Beyond

The silver screen offers a dazzling escape into fantastical worlds and thrilling adventures. But even the most epic blockbuster can have its flaws – shaky special effects, illogical plot holes, and characters who seem more like action figures than actual people. Here's how to use wit to navigate these cinematic mishaps:

* The Special Effects Shenanigans: CGI has come a long way, but sometimes the special effects fall short of spectacular. A witty remark about the unconvincing visuals can add humor to a scene that might otherwise take itself too seriously.

* Example: "Pretty sure that dragon looks like it was modeled out of Play-Doh. Maybe they should have hired a few more animators – that fire-breathing scene looked more like a birthday candle on the fritz."

* The Physics-Defying Feats: Action movies often feature characters defying the laws of physics with gravity-bending leaps and superhuman feats. A playful jab at these unrealistic stunts can add humor to the high-octane action.

* Example: "Did that hero just jump off a skyscraper and land unscathed? Pretty sure even a cat wouldn't survive that fall.

Maybe they should have consulted a physics textbook before filming that scene."

* The Bland Dialogue, Epic Delivery: Action heroes often deliver their lines with stoic determination, even when the dialogue itself is less than stellar. A witty observation about the mismatch between acting and script can be a way to add humor to the viewing experience.

* Example: "That one-liner was about as deep as a puddle. But hey, at least the actor delivered it with the intensity of a Shakespearean monologue. Maybe they should have hired a better screenwriter – those muscles deserve better lines."

Roasting the Classics (with Respect): Even the most beloved classics can have moments that seem outdated or melodramatic by today's standards. A gentle roast, delivered with respect for the film's historical significance, can add a layer of humor to your viewing experience.

* The Dramatic Declarations of Love: Classic romance films often feature grand gestures and overly dramatic declarations of love. A playful jab at these outdated expressions of affection can add humor without diminishing the film's charm.

* Example: "Did that hero just serenade his love interest from a gondola in Venice? Talk about cheesy! Maybe they should have just swiped right on Tinder – seems a bit more realistic for the modern age."

* The Villainous Clichés: Classic villains often fall into predictable stereotypes – the mustache-twirling megalomaniac or the power-hungry mad scientist. A witty remark about these villainous tropes can add humor to their nefarious schemes.

* Example: "Is that villain stroking a white cat again? Seems like they missed the handbook on 'Basic Villain Clichés.' Maybe

they should invest in a turtleneck and a brooding monologue – that always seems to work."

Turning Movie Magic into Witty Commentary

By incorporating wit into your movie-watching experience, you can become a master of cinematic critique. You'll learn to appreciate the humor in the action-packed, find amusement in the predictable, and expose the absurdity of the over-the-top. Remember, your witty remarks should be delivered with a playful spirit and an appreciation for the movie magic you're enjoying. So, grab your popcorn, dim the lights, and unleash your inner film critic with a touch of wit!

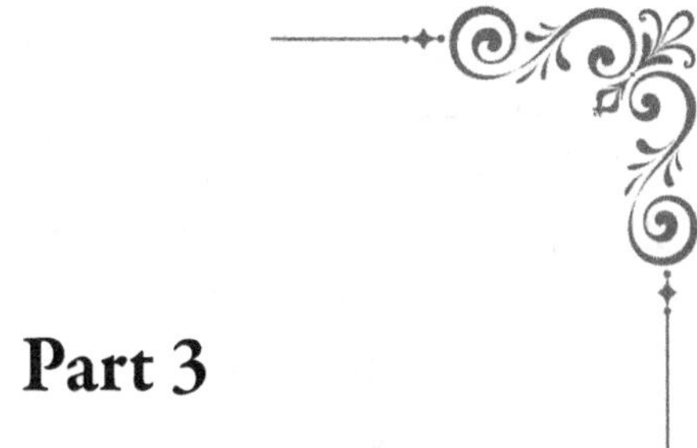

Part 3

The Streaming Service Smackdown: Finding Humor in the Binge-Watching Bonanza

Streaming services have revolutionized entertainment, offering a vast library of content at our fingertips. But with great choice comes great responsibility (and the potential for some serious couch potato-ing). Here's how to use wit to navigate the world of streaming and find humor in the endless scroll:

* The Spoiler Slayers: The internet is a minefield for spoilers, and accidentally stumbling upon a plot twist can ruin the viewing experience. A witty remark about spoiler culture can acknowledge the frustration while still keeping things light.

* Example: "Just saw a tweet that basically spoiled the entire season finale! Thanks, internet. Maybe I should invest in a social media detox while I binge-watch this show – seems like the only way to avoid spoilers these days."

* The Never-Ending Queue: With so many shows to choose from, the queue can become an overwhelming beast. A playful jab at your ever-expanding watchlist can acknowledge the struggle of choosing what to watch next.

* Example: "My watchlist is longer than a grocery store receipt! Maybe I should just hire a professional curator to sort

through this mess. How about a genre roulette wheel? Surprise me, streaming gods!"

* The Cliffhanger Catastrophe: Streaming services love cliffhangers, leaving you desperate to hit play on the next episode. A witty remark about the show's cliffhanger tactics can acknowledge the frustration while also building anticipation for what comes next.

* Example: "Did they just leave me hanging on that cliffhanger? That's cruel and unusual punishment! Maybe this show should come with a warning label – 'Guaranteed to induce binge-watching and emotional distress.'"

Roasting Your Fellow Binge-Watchers (the Kindred Spirits Kind):

* The Sleep-Deprived Streamer: Binge-watching can lead to late nights and bleary eyes. A gentle roast of your friend's sleep-deprived state can be a way to acknowledge the struggle and encourage a healthy dose of shut-eye.

* Example: "Whoa, those dark circles under your eyes are starting to form their own solar system! Maybe you should prioritize sleep over streaming for a night. Unless, of course, you're aiming for the 'Ultimate Binge-Watcher' badge – dark circles and all."

* The Prediction Pro: We all love trying to guess what will happen next in a show. A playful jab at your friend's (possibly way off) predictions can add humor to the viewing experience.

* Example: "Did you just predict that the butler did it? Again? Maybe you should invest in a crystal ball – your detective skills seem a bit rusty (or maybe wildly inaccurate)."

Turning Streaming into Witty Commentary

By using wit in this way, you can become a master of navigating the streaming landscape. You'll learn to appreciate the humor in the struggle, find amusement in the overwhelming choices, and expose the absurdity of cliffhangers designed to keep you glued to the screen. Remember, your witty remarks should be delivered with a playful spirit and a love for the stories you're streaming. So, grab your remote, settle in for your next binge-watch, and unleash your inner streaming savant with a touch of wit!

Part 4

The Music Maelstrom: Turning Up the Volume on Witty Commentary

Music is a powerful force that can evoke emotions, inspire creativity, and get your feet tapping. But even the most dedicated audiophile can find themselves facing moments of questionable lyrics, overused autotune, and musical genres that leave them scratching their heads. Fear not, music lovers (and music loathers)! With your newly honed wit, you can dissect these moments with humor and find amusement in the ever-evolving world of music.

* The Lyrical Landfill: Some song lyrics can be, well, a little nonsensical. A playful jab at the questionable rhymes or metaphors can add humor to your listening experience.

* Example: "Is that singer comparing love to a burnt piece of toast? Not sure that's the most romantic metaphor. Maybe they should invest in a thesaurus – seems like their vocabulary is stuck on repeat."

* The Auto-Tune Avalanche: Auto-tune can be a powerful tool for pitch correction, but sometimes it's used a little too liberally. A witty remark about the robotic vocals can add humor to a song that might otherwise take itself too seriously.

* Example: "Pretty sure that singer sounds more like a robot than a human being. Maybe they should lay off the auto-tune – a little imperfection can be a good thing (or at least more interesting to listen to)."

* The Genre Gamble: The world of music offers a vast array of genres, from the soothing sounds of classical to the pulsating beats of electronic dance music. A lighthearted roast of a genre you're not particularly fond of can be a way to acknowledge your musical preferences (and maybe spark a friendly debate with fellow music lovers).

* Example: "Is this polka music still a thing? Pretty sure it peaked sometime in the 1800s. Maybe I should stick to my head-banging anthems – at least they get my heart racing (in a good way)."

Roasting Your Fellow Music Enthusiasts (The Harmonious Kind):

* The One-Hit Wonder Worshipper: We all have those songs that get stuck in our heads, even if they're objectively not that great. A gentle roast of your friend's love for a cheesy pop song can add humor to your shared listening experience.

* Example: "Is this song playing on repeat again? Pretty sure I've heard it enough times to sing along backwards. Maybe you should invest in a new playlist – this one is starting to wear thin (like a really bad pair of jeans)."

* The Earbud Evangelist: Some people love sharing their music with the world, blasting their earbuds at full volume on public transportation. A playful jab at their musical evangelism can be a way to acknowledge the intrusion while keeping things light.

* Example: "Is that the entire soundtrack of the apocalypse playing through your headphones? Maybe you should consider investing in noise-canceling headphones for everyone else's sake – not everyone shares your taste in heavy metal."

Turning Melodies into Witty Commentary

By using wit in this way, you can become a master of musical critique. You'll learn to appreciate the humor in the nonsensical, find amusement in the overused, and expose the absurdity of genres that just aren't your cup of tea (or genre, as the case may be). Remember, your witty remarks should be delivered with a playful spirit and a love for the music you're engaging with, even if you're gently roasting it. So, crank up the volume, put on your favorite (or least favorite) tunes, and unleash your inner music critic with a touch of wit!

Chapter 4: The Art of Wit in the Social Jungle

Part 1

So far, you've mastered the art of witty roasting in everyday situations, from navigating social awkwardness to dissecting pop culture trends. But the social jungle extends far beyond the confines of your living room or the familiar faces on your screen. This chapter will equip you with the tools to use wit effectively in various social settings, transforming you into a master of witty conversation.

Witty Workplace Wisdom: Keeping it Professional (and Hilarious)

The workplace can be a breeding ground for stress, deadlines, and the occasional soul-crushing meeting. But fear not, corporate warriors! A touch of wit can lighten the mood, build camaraderie with colleagues, and even impress your boss (in a good way). Here's how to use humor strategically in the professional sphere:

* The Watercooler Witticisms: Water cooler moments are a chance to connect with colleagues and unwind after a long day. A witty observation about a current event or a playful jab at a shared workplace woe can be a great conversation starter.

* Example: "Did you see that news story about the office supply delivery gone wrong? Talk about a paper jam of epic proportions! Maybe we should invest in carrier pigeons for our

inter-office memo needs – seems like a more reliable option these days."

* The Meeting Merriment: Meetings can be long and tedious, but a well-timed witty remark can lighten the mood and keep everyone engaged. However, remember to strike a balance – your wit shouldn't derail the meeting or offend any colleagues.

* Example: "Okay, so that presentation was about as exciting as watching paint dry. Maybe we should all take a coffee break and come back with some fresh ideas – and maybe a gallon of caffeine to keep us awake for the next round." (Use this sparingly and only in a safe work environment!).

* The Self-Deprecating Savior: We've all made mistakes at work. A touch of self-deprecating humor can acknowledge your error and show you can laugh at yourself. This can be a disarming tactic and help you navigate an awkward situation.

* Example: "Wow, that spreadsheet is a complete mess! Pretty sure I need a crash course in basic math before I unleash this monstrosity on the world. Maybe someone can volunteer to decipher my financial hieroglyphics?"

Witty Social Gatherings: The Life of the Party (Without Being Annoying)

Social gatherings are a chance to connect with friends, new acquaintances, and maybe even make a lasting impression. Wit can be a powerful tool in these settings, but remember, the goal is to be charming and entertaining, not the obnoxious center of attention.

* The Icebreaker Inquiry: Walking into a party full of strangers can be nerve-wracking. A witty icebreaker question can spark a conversation and show off your playful side.

* Example: "Is this the 'awkward silence' section of the party, or am I just in the wrong place? Just kidding! But seriously, what are the chances we both secretly came here dressed as our spirit animals?"

* The Group Conversation Guru: Group conversations can be tricky, and sometimes you need a witty remark to keep the conversation flowing or steer it in a more interesting direction.

* Example: "Did someone say 'cheese'? Because this conversation is starting to feel a bit stale. Maybe we should play a game of 'Would You Rather?' – always a good way to get things interesting (and maybe a little heated)."

* The Social Media Savvy Wit: Social media can be a platform to share witty observations and connect with your online network. A funny caption or a playful comment can show off your personality and make your posts more engaging.

* Example: "Just spent 20 minutes trying to untangle my headphones. Pretty sure I've achieved a level of frustration that should be classified as an Olympic sport. #FirstWorldProblems #SendWine"

Remember: Wit in social settings is all about balance. Be playful, be observant, and be mindful of your audience. A well-timed witty remark can leave a lasting impression, but an insensitive jab can damage relationships. So, use your newfound wit wisely, and you'll be the life of the party (without being annoying) in no time!

Part 2

Witty Encounters: Navigating Dates and Family Gatherings

The social jungle extends beyond the office and casual parties. Here's how to use wit to navigate potentially awkward situations like dates and family gatherings:

The Dating Do's and Don'ts of Wit:

* The Playful Poke: A first date can be nerve-wracking, but a lighthearted jab at your own nervousness or a playful observation about the setting can break the ice.

* Example: "So, this is awkward, right? I'm pretty sure I forgot how to hold a conversation that doesn't involve sweatpants and takeout menus. But hey, at least the restaurant has good lighting – perfect for hiding my first-date jitters."

* The Shared Laughter Strategy: Finding humor in a common experience, like a spilled drink or a menu mishap, can create a sense of connection and ease tension on a date.

* Example: "Is the universe trying to tell us something with this never-ending stream of napkins? Maybe we should just switch to writing our order in ketchup – seems like a less messy option at this point."

* The Self-Awareness Safety Net: A touch of self-deprecating humor can acknowledge your flaws or quirks and show you're not taking yourself too seriously.

* Example: "I may have ordered the spiciest dish on the menu without realizing it. Pretty sure I'm sweating more than a nervous high schooler giving a valedictorian speech. Maybe you could share your water – and your sense of humor – with a spice-challenged soul?"

Family Gatherings: Keeping Things Light with Wit

* The Political Minefield: Family gatherings can sometimes lead to heated discussions, especially on sensitive topics like politics. A witty remark can lighten the mood and steer the conversation in a different direction.

* Example: "Uh oh, I smell a potential political debate brewing! Maybe we should all take a break and discuss the most important topic of the day – what's for dessert? Changing the world can wait – chocolate cake cannot." (Use this with caution and only if you know your family dynamic can handle it!)

* The Quirky Aunt/Uncle Challenge: Family gatherings often involve eccentric relatives. A playful jab at their unique personality traits can be a way to acknowledge their quirks with affection.

* Example: "Aunt Edna, is that a new hat, or did you win a prize in a disco ball competition? You always know how to make an entrance – and blind everyone in the process with all that sparkle!" (Of course, be mindful of the relative's sense of humor!)

* The Childhood Embarrassment Exposé: Family gatherings often involve reminiscing about childhood memories. A witty remark about your own embarrassing childhood moments can

show you can laugh at yourself and encourage others to share their funny stories.

* Example: "Remember that time I tried to dye my hair green with Kool-Aid? Pretty sure it looked more like a science experiment gone wrong than a trendy hairstyle. Thank goodness for the invention of hats – and the merciful passage of time."

Remember: The key to using wit in these situations is to be respectful, even when teasing. A touch of humor can go a long way in navigating potentially awkward moments and strengthening relationships with loved ones.

Part 3

The Art of the Comeback: Turning Awkward into Awesome
Even the most skilled social navigators will encounter awkward moments. But fear not, wit warriors! A well-timed comeback can turn an embarrassing situation into a hilarious one, leaving everyone laughing (including you). Here's how to use wit to deflect awkwardness and emerge victorious:

* The Self-deprecating Dodge: Sometimes, the best way to deflect an awkward comment is to laugh at yourself. A touch of self-deprecation can disarm the situation and show you can take a joke.

* Example: "Wow, that was a smooth move – about as smooth as a baby penguin on ice skates. Maybe I should stick to witty banter and leave the acrobatics to the professionals."

* The Playful Pivot: An awkward comment can derail a conversation. A playful pivot can help you steer the conversation in a different direction without dwelling on the awkwardness.

* Example: "That reminds me of the funniest thing that happened to me the other day..." (and launch into a lighthearted anecdote that steers the conversation away from the awkward moment).

* The Witty Reversal: Sometimes, you can turn an awkward comment on its head with a witty reversal. This can be a

disarming tactic that leaves the other person speechless (in a good way).

* Example: "Is that your way of saying I have a forgettable face? Well, at least I'm memorable for something, even if it's just my terrible memory!" (Use this with caution and only if the situation feels right!)

Remember: The goal of a comeback isn't to humiliate the other person, but to deflect awkwardness and keep the conversation flowing. A lighthearted and playful approach is always best.

The Art of the Compliment: The Power of Witty Appreciation

Wit isn't just about making people laugh, it's also about making them feel good. A witty compliment can be a powerful tool for building relationships and showing genuine appreciation. Here's how to use wit to compliment in a way that's both memorable and sincere:

* The Specific Shout-Out: A generic compliment can feel insincere. A specific compliment that highlights a person's unique talent or accomplishment is much more impactful.

* Example: "I love how you can always find the humor in a situation! You're basically a walking stress ball deflator – with the added bonus of being incredibly witty."

* The Playful Juxtaposition: A compliment doesn't have to be overly serious. A playful juxtaposition can be a way to show appreciation while keeping things light.

* Example: "Your creativity is truly out of this world! Maybe you should give up your day job and become a professional astronaut – designing spaceships would definitely be a good use of your talents (and your impressive sense of style)."

* The Self-deprecating Setup: A touch of self-deprecation can set the stage for a compliment that feels more genuine.

* Example: "I wish I could be as organized as you are! My desk is a constant disaster zone. But hey, at least I can appreciate your immaculate workspace – it's truly a thing of beauty (and a source of inspiration for this clutter queen)."

Remember: A well-timed compliment delivered with wit can leave a lasting impression and show the people you care about that you appreciate them.

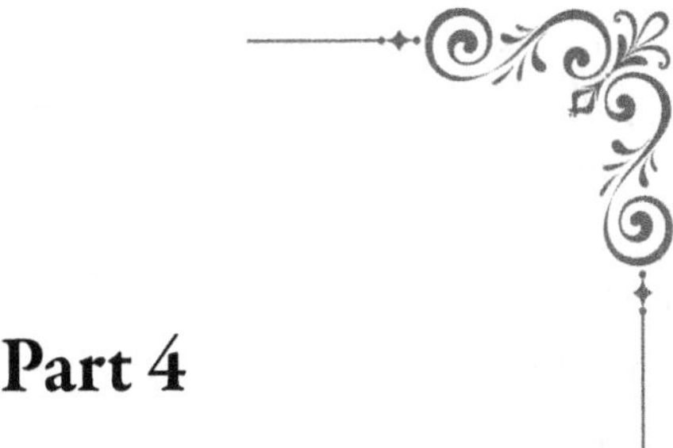

Part 4

The Long Game: Honing Your Witty Arsenal

Wit isn't a magic trick you master overnight. It's a skill that requires practice, observation, and a healthy dose of self-awareness. Here are some tips to help you hone your witty arsenal and become a master conversationalist:

* Become a Keen Observer: Pay attention to the world around you. Notice the quirks of everyday life, the funny turns of phrase people use, and the unexpected connections between seemingly disparate ideas. This will give you a treasure trove of material to draw from when crafting your witty remarks.

* Embrace the Power of Play: Don't be afraid to experiment and have fun with language. Play with words, try out different phrasings, and see what makes you laugh. The more playful your approach, the more likely you are to come up with something truly witty.

* Learn from the Masters: Pay attention to comedians, writers, and other witty individuals you admire. See how they use humor, timing, and wordplay to create laughter. Analyze what works and what doesn't, and incorporate these learnings into your own style.

* Practice Makes Perfect: The more you use wit in everyday conversation, the more comfortable you'll become. Don't be

afraid to take risks and try out new jokes (even if they sometimes fall flat). The more you practice, the sharper your wit will become.

* Embrace the Fail: Not every witty remark will land perfectly. That's okay! Learn from your mistakes, dust yourself off, and try again. Sometimes, the most memorable moments come from what doesn't quite go according to plan.

Remember: Wit is a journey, not a destination. Embrace the process of learning, growing, and occasionally failing. With dedication and a playful spirit, you'll transform yourself into a master of witty conversation, leaving a trail of laughter in your wake.

Bonus Tip: Wit is a powerful tool, but it should always be used with kindness and respect. Avoid humor that insults, belittles, or excludes others. The goal is to create laughter and connection, not division.

So, go forth, social warriors, and unleash your wit upon the world! Remember, a little humor can go a long way in brightening your day, making others smile, and navigating the ever-unpredictable social jungle.

Chapter 5: Witty Wins in the Wild World of Work

Part 1

The workplace can be a complex ecosystem, filled with deadlines, meetings, and the occasional office nemesis (we've all had one). But fear not, working warriors! Wit can be a powerful tool in your professional arsenal, helping you navigate tricky situations, build rapport with colleagues, and even impress your boss (in a good way). In this chapter, we'll delve deeper into the art of using humor strategically to win in the wild world of work.

The Conference Room Conundrums: Delivering Witty Wisdom in Meetings

Meetings are a fact of professional life, and they can sometimes feel like an eternity trapped in a room with flickering fluorescent lights and endless PowerPoint presentations. Here's how to use wit to liven things up and contribute meaningfully:

* The Engaging Opener: Start your participation with a witty remark related to the meeting topic. This can grab attention, demonstrate your knowledge of the subject matter, and set a positive tone.

* Example: "So, the agenda says we're discussing 'maximizing productivity.' If anyone has any secret strategies to avoid falling asleep during these marathon meetings, now's the time to share them! But seriously, I'm curious to hear some innovative ideas..."

* The Questionable Slide Savior: Let's face it, some presentation slides can be, well, boring. A witty observation about a confusing graph or an overly technical term can lighten the mood and spark a discussion.

* Example: "Is this chart supposed to be a work of modern art, or am I missing something here? Maybe we should invest in a translator for this jargon – these acronyms are starting to give me a headache." (Use this sparingly and only if the slide is truly confusing!)

* The Disagreement Diffuser: Disagreements are inevitable in meetings. A witty remark can help acknowledge the differing viewpoints and steer the conversation towards a solution.

* Example: "Okay, things are getting a little heated in here! Maybe we all need a coffee break to cool down and come back with some fresh ideas (and maybe a sense of humor). How about we table this discussion for now and revisit it with clear minds (and full stomachs)?"

Remember: The goal of wit in meetings is to be engaged, not disruptive. Use humor to contribute to the conversation, not derail it.

Part 2

The Email Etiquette of Wit: Striking the Right Tone in Electronic Communication

Emails are a cornerstone of professional communication, but they can also be breeding grounds for misunderstandings and misinterpretations. Here's how to use wit in your emails to add personality, build rapport, and ensure your message lands as intended:

* The Subject Line Switcheroo: A witty subject line can pique the recipient's curiosity and encourage them to open your email. However, avoid anything that could be perceived as unprofessional or sarcastic.

* Example: "Project Update: It's Not on Fire (Yet!)" (Use this with caution and only with colleagues you know well!)

* The Lighthearted Opener: Start your email with a friendly and playful greeting. A witty remark related to a shared experience or a current event can break the ice and set a positive tone.

* Example: "Hope you survived the meeting marathon yesterday! I swear, we discussed enough spreadsheets to wallpaper a small office. But hey, at least we can all bond over our shared caffeine dependence."

* The Self-Deprecating Savior: Making a small mistake in an email happens to the best of us. A touch of self-deprecating humor can acknowledge your error and show you can laugh at yourself.

* Example: "Just realized I attached the wrong document to my previous email. ♀ Please forgive my senior moment – my brain is clearly still on vacation mode. Here's the correct file (hopefully)!"

Remember: Wit in emails is a balancing act. Keep it lighthearted, professional, and avoid anything that could be misinterpreted as insensitive or rude.

The Art of the Elevator Pitch: Delivering Witty Wins in Short Bursts

The elevator pitch: a short, impactful statement summarizing your idea or project. A touch of wit can make your pitch memorable and leave a lasting impression.

* The Intriguing Intro: Start your pitch with a thought-provoking question or a surprising statistic that grabs the listener's attention.

* Example: "Did you know that 80% of office workers dream of escaping their cubicles? Well, I have an idea that can make those dreams a reality..."

* The Witty Wordplay: A creative turn of phrase or a clever metaphor can make your pitch more engaging and memorable.

* Example: "Think of our product as the Swiss Army Knife of productivity tools – it can tackle any task you throw its way with efficiency and ease."

* The Confident Conclusion: End your pitch with a confident statement that leaves the listener wanting to learn more.

* Example: "So, are you ready to ditch the drudgery and embrace a new era of productivity? Let's chat about how this can revolutionize your workflow."

Remember: The key to a witty elevator pitch is brevity and impact. Use humor strategically to grab attention, showcase your idea, and leave a lasting impression.

By using wit in these strategic ways, you can transform yourself into a workplace warrior, navigating the professional jungle with humor, confidence, and a touch of charm.

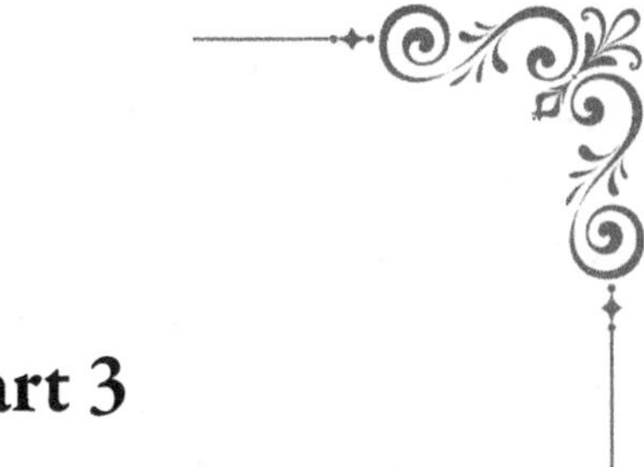

Part 3

The Office Ordeals: Using Wit to Conquer Common Workplace Woes

The office can be a treasure trove of (sometimes hilarious) situations. Here's how to use wit to navigate common workplace struggles and emerge victorious (and maybe even a little entertained):

* The Technical Fail Fiasco: Technology can be our best friend and worst enemy at work. A witty remark about a computer crash or a malfunctioning printer can acknowledge the frustration while keeping things light.

* Example: "Is it just me, or is this printer possessed by the ghost of a disgruntled office worker? Maybe we should invest in carrier pigeons for our inter-departmental memos – seems like a more reliable option at this point."

* The Endless Errand Expedition: We've all been tasked with seemingly pointless errands. A playful jab at the absurdity of the request can show your willingness to help while acknowledging the questionable nature of the errand.

* Example: "So, my next mission is to find the office supply unicorn – a stapler that actually staples and doesn't jam every five seconds. Wish me luck on this epic quest! But seriously, on my way to conquer the supply closet..."

* The Coworker Catastrophe: Even the best workplaces have challenging colleagues. A witty remark about a coworker's quirks (delivered with kindness, of course) can help you bond over shared frustrations and create a sense of camaraderie.

* Example: "Did Michael just call himself a 'power napper' again? Pretty sure that's just a fancy term for sleeping on the job. But hey, at least he's enthusiastic – even if his enthusiasm involves catching some midday Zzzs." (Use this with caution and only with colleagues you know well!)

Remember: Wit in these situations should be used to create humor, not negativity. A lighthearted approach can diffuse tension, build relationships, and make even the most mundane tasks a little more enjoyable.

The Art of the Farewell: Leaving a Lasting Witty Impression

Whether you're moving on to a new opportunity or simply leaving for the day, a witty farewell can leave a positive lasting impression.

* The Playful Sign-Off: End your email or in-person goodbye with a playful remark that reflects your personality.

* Example: "Signing off for the day! May your commute be traffic-free, your inbox manageable, and your coffee never lukewarm. Until tomorrow, colleagues!"

* The Future-Focused Farewell: If you're leaving the company, a witty remark about your future plans can acknowledge the change while expressing gratitude for your time there.

* Example: "So long, farewell, and thanks for all the fish (and the office shenanigans)! I'm off to pursue new horizons – maybe I'll finally have time to tackle that ever-growing to-do list at home (wish me luck!)."

Remember: A witty farewell shows you can leave with grace and a sense of humor. It's a chance to end your time on a positive note and build lasting connections with your colleagues.

By using wit in these creative ways, you can navigate the ever-changing landscape of the workplace with humor, resilience, and a touch of charm. You'll not only survive the office jungle, you'll thrive in it, leaving a trail of laughter and positive memories in your wake.

Part 4

The Final Word: Wit Beyond the Workplace

The art of wit isn't confined to the walls of your office. The skills you've honed in the professional jungle can translate to all areas of your life. Here are some parting thoughts on how wit can enrich your experiences beyond the workplace:

* Wit as a Social Currency: Wit can be a powerful tool for building rapport and making new friends. A well-timed joke or a playful observation can break the ice and create a sense of connection.

* Wit as a Creative Spark: Wit can fuel your creativity. Playful wordplay and unexpected connections can spark new ideas, whether you're brainstorming solutions to a problem or simply coming up with a funny caption for your latest social media post.

* Wit as a Confidence Booster: Being witty can boost your confidence and make you feel more comfortable in social situations. When you know you can make people laugh, it can be easier to put yourself out there and connect with others.

* Wit as a Stress Reliever: Laughter is the best medicine, and wit can be a powerful stress reliever. A funny observation or a witty comeback can help you lighten the mood and navigate challenging situations with a smile.

Remember: Wit is a journey, not a destination. Embrace the process of learning, growing, and occasionally failing. With practice, self-awareness, and a dash of playfulness, you can become a master of wit, leaving a trail of laughter and positive connections wherever you go.

So, the next time you find yourself in a social situation, a work meeting, or even just facing down a malfunctioning printer, remember the power of wit. With a touch of humor, a sprinkle of creativity, and a kind heart, you can transform everyday encounters into memorable moments, leaving everyone around you smiling.

Conclusion

> NOW, ARMED WITH THE knowledge in this book, you should be a master of wit, ready to conquer any social situation with laughter. Just remember, with great wit comes great responsibility. Don't be the life of the party who accidentally sets the punch bowl on fire (metaphorically or literally). Use your newfound wit wisely, and you'll find yourself not just surviving social gatherings, but thriving in them. After all, laughter is contagious, and who wouldn't want to be the carrier of a hilarious strain?

> BUT A WORD OF CAUTION: excessive wit can have side effects. You might find yourself quoting puns at funerals, making your grandma snort her prune juice. Moderation is key, folks. Besides, a little mystery keeps things interesting. You don't want to be the predictable joke machine at every party. Leave some room for others to chime in with their own witty remarks (unless they're truly awful, then feel free to unleash your comedic arsenal).

> SO GO FORTH, WITTY warriors! Spread laughter, build connections, and remember, the world needs more people who can find humor in a stapler malfunction (because let's be honest, staplers are the true villains of the office). Now, if you'll excuse

me, I have a date with a thesaurus – gotta expand that vocabulary to keep those witty remarks fresh!

About the Author

The Writer Ullu is a name that resonates with uniqueness and creativity in the literary world. Known for their captivating stories that blend fun, facts, and the bizarre, The Writer Ullu has carved a niche that stands out. Recently, they have ventured into the realm of ghostwriting under the same name, adding another dimension to their repertoire. Alongside this, they have founded their own publishing house, D-COOP (Dark-Community Of Owl Publishing), which promises to be a sanctuary for unconventional and intriguing narratives. The content produced by The Writer Ullu, now under the banner of D-COOP, offers readers a delightful mix of entertainment and education, often exploring the strange and unusual. This new chapter in their career not only broadens their creative horizons but also provides a platform for other voices to emerge, all while maintaining the distinctive charm and originality that defines The Writer Ullu.

Read more at www.dcoopbooks.rf.gd.

www.ingramcontent.com/pod-product-compliance
Lightning Source LLC
Chambersburg PA
CBHW061618130726

47996CB00003B/1030